CONFLICT: OUR MOST PRECIOUS RESOURCE

It's always been interesting to me that conflict and play seem to go hand in hand. Wherever there is play, conflict usually emerges in some way, shape or form. Call me silly but I've learned to love it. The name-calling, pushing, brawling, etc., all leave a bad taste in our mouths but conflict can have some positive things that come out of it if a solid conflict resolution process follows it.

All too often, children learn not to resolve their conflicts. Rather, they are taught to focus on the events of the conflict and then an expert or authority figure will come in and solve the problem for them. But this is no resolution; it's a patch. When the same problem pops up again and again between the same people the typical response is to escalate the consequences: lecture, time-out, written response, call to parents, conference with parents… we know that every school has an escalation protocol for recurring problems. Some are well-meaning and some are punitive. Unfortunately, too many times we don't trust our children enough to handle their own problems and decide their own solutions. Our actions show that we think that they lack the skills to resolve conflicts.

Fast forward ten years into high school and the lack of conflict resolution skills results in even more problems. Not only have they learned that the problems they have with others will be solved by a higher authority, they learn that they will be judged. It leaves scores of students in a pretty hopeless place-- powerless, without a choice or a voice. It's like they are in some kind of limbo that replays the scenes of the conflict while they wait for someone to come and solve the problem for them.

A BENEFIT OF CONFLICT

Covey had a theory about the difference between successful people in the past and successful people of today. The old paradigm of independence demonstrated how successful people could scratch and claw their way over the backs of others and get to the top. Nowadays, the sum of the whole is greater than the individual parts. That is, what we can do together vastly surpasses what we can achieve on our own. Case in point, I'm citing Covey right now. Without his work, and the work of others, I would have needed to develop some very basic concepts before getting to this point. The bottom line: Your success within an organization depends on how well you work with other people. It is therefore vital for all of us to know how to work with other people. For a relationship to be successful, the partners need to know how to work with each other. And, in order for an organization to be successful beyond their own level, (i.e. management, administration, frontline), a spirit of cooperation and teamwork needs to be firmly rooted throughout.

LET THE CHILDREN PLAY!

My daughter went to a play-based cooperative preschool. Most people understand that a "cooperative" type of preschool means that parents work at the school as part of the staff. Not many truly understand what is meant by "play-based". At first glance, a play-based preschool is mayhem with a bunch of activity centers set up so that children might choose what they want to explore without a set curriculum being forced onto them.

Sounds pretty much like a hippie commune, doesn't it?

One objection that inevitably arises at a play-based school is "the students aren't learning anything so they won't be prepared for Kindergarten". While many preschools pride themselves on producing children that can recite and write their ABCs, count to ten in multiple languages, identify shapes and colors and perform some impressive advanced tasks for a 3 – 5 year-old, the play-based kids seem to be left behind. You can tell who they are when they get to Kindergarten because they never learned to march in line like the academically advanced students.

Conflict is at the heart of every play-based school. Conflict is what drives the learning process. It *is* the curriculum. The activity centers are a conduit to bring students who are age-appropriately playing side-by-side into a soft collision with those around them. When these little worlds collide at a play-based center, students learn appropriate ways to express their emotions, avoid causing physical harm and negotiate a solution. How many adults can do that for themselves?

The basic premise behind a play-based pre-school is to give children the tools they need to resolve their own conflicts so that they can negotiate the Kindergarten and elementary school arena effectively. Once they have conflict resolution skills in their repertoire they can focus on abstract language and math concepts at a time when it is age-appropriate to do so. In contrast, children who have an academic head start will be floundering on the playground and the social arena because those concepts aren't being taught and they never will be.

Remember: A chain is only as strong as its weakest link.

Every time we engage with others there is the potential for conflict to arise. When conflict arises, we must necessarily improvise, that is, use the practiced responses we have learned from experience to answer the challenge in front of us. If we know some basic maneuvers and practice them and learn more advanced maneuvers and practice them, we will have improved our chances of not falling into frustration. We thrive. The point is, we have a choice to either address a conflict with a practiced and polished response or we can get frustrated, give up and let it crush us.

Conflict presents an opportunity for growth. If we address conflict the right way, with an attitude of willingness and openness to learning, we thrive. Conflict can actually benefit us. It challenges us to be better. It proves to us that there is hope; there is usually a way to work around the problem. Finally, we feel engaged in life and empowered to create our own destiny. On the flip side, when we don't view conflict as an opportunity and we run away from it, let it go unresolved or let others resolve it, we learn hopelessness, powerlessness, fear and become closed off to the possibilities around us. We put our destiny in the hands of others and blame them when things don't go our way.

THE CASE FOR CONFLICT RESOLUTION IN CURRICULUM

With few exceptions, conflict resolution is given a back seat in play spaces of the country. When a problem breaks out on a school playground, there is usually a huge mob of onlookers around. All play stops. The yard supervisors (think of them as the "peacekeepers") may come together to separate students, find out what happened and make people apologize or maybe send them to the office for disciplinary action. Little is done at all to get to a resolution of the conflict. False apologies are exchanged and the next day the same two are back at it again for the same reasons. I think of this as "meatball surgery" for obvious reasons. The patients get patched up quickly with little more than gauze and ointment and then they are sent back to the war.

Handling conflict, resolving it to our liking, makes us feel good about ourselves. For this reason alone, an efficient and effective model of conflict resolution that both empowers and validates conflicting parties to resolve their conflict in a manner so that it doesn't erupt again is necessary and prudent. Teaching conflict resolution in schools and on playgrounds will do much more than lower the reactivity of the student body during recess. It will help people at a young age internalize a coping mechanism that will serve them in their daily lives as they face tougher and tougher challenges.

Why aren't our young people being offered something more substantial?

Are we really going to let our children grow up to learn advanced mathematical concepts, how to structure the perfect essay, become business professionals and enter into Ph.D. programs but never learn how to resolve their own conflicts in a satisfying way? These emotionally unaware adults will be ill-equipped to handle problems handed down from previous generations such as global climate change, international diplomacy issues, economic strife and dwindling natural resources. God forbid we stock our world with a bunch of world leaders who cry foul and treat each other disrespectfully during high-level negotiations and then run out of the room when they don't get their way. Our generation is doing all it can to kick the can down the road. The emotional awareness gained through the ability to resolve one's own conflicts is worth investing a little extra time teaching conflict resolution techniques in the play spaces when and where the need arises.

A BETTER WAY TO RESOLVE CONFLICT

The Middle East conflict was said to have been the result of two brothers, Isaac and Ismael, fighting over their birthright. Ismael was the firstborn son of Abraham but, because he was born of a concubine, was not treated as the rightful heir. Abraham, being the father and authority figure, decided the outcome.

It didn't stop the two sons from arguing. The descendants of Isaac and Ismael have been fighting ever since. If only Abraham had taken the time to teach them to solve their problems rather than decide for them.

Most conflict resolution is done the same way. Two conflicting parties go to an authority figure who presides over the squabble, listens to each side of the story and then decides the outcome. The parties in conflict are told what to do and what terms they are going to accept. They have no real say in the resolution. The mediator listens to the convolutions of each story and attempts to make sense of it. The mediator does a lot of work while the people who are in the actual conflict sit back and relax until judgment is handed down. Usually that judgment is unsatisfactory and doesn't address the original issue. It does nothing to validate the emotions of the individuals actually involved.

The ReST Method of Conflict Resolution is different. The mediator doesn't hear both sides of the story but does set guidelines for the two conflicting parties to hear each other. The mediator doesn't decide the outcome but he/she does judge whether it is a strong resolution. Do you see where this is going? Can you picture yourself relaxing when you need to get involved with a conflict in your classroom or on your playground? The ReST Method promises just that: as a mediator, you will not be doing the work that it takes to resolve the conflict.

Here is what I promise you will get by learning and applying the ReST Method of Conflict Resolution:

a) You will improve your occupational prospects as an educator, supervisor/manager, counselor, babysitter or daycare provider.
b) You will learn to use a method of conflict resolution that ensures the same conflict won't reignite between the same parties.
c) You will gain confidence in your ability to resolve conflicts.
d) You will learn techniques of effective communication that will improve your self-esteem and your value to others.
e) You will empower those you work with to achieve success in their interpersonal interactions and beyond.
f) You will boost your confidence, feel love, improve your whole life and take those you mediate on the same journey.
g) You will save time and money by applying these techniques.

If the ReST Method of Conflict Resolution had been known back in Abraham's time, maybe we wouldn't have the Middle East conflict as we know it today.

ABOUT ME

This book is the result of many years of working with students, from pre-school to high school, on the playground, in therapy and in the classroom. I began as a daycare professional, running day camps and childcare programs for different public and private organizations. After some time I studied to become a therapist, working with middle school and high school students. Years later, I went back to school and obtained my multi-subject elementary teaching credential. In every situation, conflict resolution skills have been an important part of my daily routine.

GOALS

I hope to accomplish a few things with this writing: First, I want to convince you that conflict represents an opportunity to make positive and lasting change. Second, I want to give you the tools to make it an easy process in whatever forum you find it necessary—school, camp, community center, recreational program, interpersonal situation or even diplomacy between warring nations. Finally, I want to open up the conversation about conflict resolution so that others may benefit from this method.

I will be talking about conflict resolution as if you are a third party mediator who is *outside*, that is, not part of the conflict. However, if you tweak these ideas, especially by applying the steps outlined in

"Effective Communication", you will also be able to apply them to your own personal conflicts as an insider.

WHAT IS THE ReST METHOD OF CONFLICT RESOLUTION???

In short, the ReST Method of Conflict Resolution is a more efficient conflict resolution method that produces long-lasting results for parties in conflict. It promises 100% satisfaction for both parties or at least that both parties will walk away feeling they both have won.

Becoming an effective mediator doesn't happen overnight. I admit that some people are able to develop mediation skills more quickly than others. Mastering them takes time and persistence. You will learn it out of necessity the more you mediate but, especially, if you are able to practice the basics as part of a daily routine. Our character is merely a collection of our habits, based upon endless repetition until the behavior becomes ingrained and forms a habit. Karen S. Deerwater, Ed.S., ("Routines That Teach", BlueSuitMom.com, 2003, webpage), outlines what it takes for parents to teach daily routines to their children:

1) Decide the behavior you expect ("You will be solving this problem")
2) Explain it in simple terms ("You will be listening to each other")
3) Be a hands-on parent ("I will be here to make sure it is happening")

These three simple steps, repeated often enough, are all it takes to develop routines that become habits.

Respect – Safety - Trust

I call it the ReST Method because it is based on creating an atmosphere of respect (R), safety (S), and trust (T) while the mediator keeps their own ego (e) out of it. There is no room for an all-knowing expert. The mediator acts more like a coach and has no ego at stake. The goal is to create an atmosphere of Respect, Safety and Trust so that the two parties in conflict can resolve *their* issue.

<u>Respect</u>

Respect creates buy-in. A person who is respected has leverage. Your goal is to get each party to respect you as well as each other. They don't have to like each other. They don't need to shake hands at the end of it. They do need to respect each other and all parts of the resolution process, especially the terms of the resolution that they agree to. Respect is something we expect but is taken for granted.

You've heard the colloquialism "dis". When someone says I've "dissed" them, it means that I've disrespected them. I've done something that another person has an issue with and it creates a social imbalance. The majority of conflicts I've dealt with began with one person dissing another. From there it escalated into something bigger. When you set 'respect' as an expectation in the resolution session, you are addressing the imbalance.

Mediation should only be done by a person that both parties can respect and who holds mutual respect for those they are mediating. You may need to create that on the spot in a heated conflict. You may be angry at someone for crossing a line but you will get nowhere by shouting in someone's face, blaming them for doing wrong or taking sides because you witnessed something. Chances are, you don't know the whole story behind a conflict. Anyone trying to mediate needs to leave their feelings behind about who's right and who's wrong.

In the heat of an argument, when insults fly, things can get confusing. Your job is to stay with the big picture and to keep everyone else on task. Don't get off on a tangent trying to follow the loose threads of a disagreement. A strong mediator can sort out the pieces of the conflict that contribute to the problem from the pieces that have no bearing on the outcome. Expect respect from all people involved. Most importantly, give respect as a way of setting the tone of the process.

Safety

People in conflict exhibit both aggressive and fearful behavior. They are being asked to come face-to-face with the other person and may not feel safe or they may burst out in violence. The mediator needs to guarantee that physical violence does not erupt during the resolution session. They must be ready to protect against aggression and lower the temperature of the two people in conflict so that aggression does not disrupt the process.

People who are exhibiting aggressive or fearful behavior are expressing anxiety. In the field of psychotherapy we are taught that anxiety and depression are like two sides of the same coin. If you think of the anxious person in conflict as in a state of depression, you tend to have more compassion for them. By creating a safe place you will lower the amount of anxiety between the two parties. Lowering the anxiety allows for each person to focus on the task at hand.

In addition, people in conflict may be putting on a brave face or a front. The mediator needs to create a place that can contain the free flow of true emotion that takes place. People need to feel that they can say what they need to say without fear of repercussion or judgment. For example, a high school age student may use profanity during a resolution session. Is it really necessary to punish her/him for that? Redirecting them to use less foul language is a way for them to feel validated and to understand some limits.

Trust

As a mediator, the trust you develop with each person brings about a state of willingness. The less you act in a manner that they can trust, the less likely they are to cooperate towards the end goal of resolving the conflict. You develop trust by taking a non-threatening, non-authoritative posture. Trust develops over time as the parties realize that the place they are in is truly safe, they have been shown respect and have been given responsibility for their own resolution. You have placed this trust in their hands. You need to let them know that you believe they can accomplish a resolution.

The small "e"

The small "e" in the ReST Method stands for "keeping your own ego out of the mediation process" as well as "downplaying the role of the expert". As the mediator of the conflict you need to act more like a coach who redirects unwanted behavior rather than an expert who has all the answers. Let's think about the difference between these two roles.

The expert pontificates in order to instruct. The coach collaborates. The expert uses a didactic method, telling students what is going on while the coach lets students discover something about the process. The expert asks questions that expect a "yes" or "no" answer while the coach asks open-ended questions. The expert follows the Sherlock Holmes model, suggesting _how to_ do something rather than the Columbo model asking _how_ they do something. The expert uses thought pattern statements (e.g. "I think…") rather than affect pattern statements (e.g. "I feel…"). The expert has a plan and gives directives (e.g. "Here's what to do…") while the coach gives suggestions (e.g. Here's what some have done…"). The expert prepares a full lesson while the coach partially structures interactions. An expert gives homework while a coach sets up personalized experiments.

The expert is someone we don't want in the resolution process. The expert is resented and, therefore, does not promote respect. The coach has a way of softening the hard questions in a way that makes the parties want to be there. The coach doesn't tell the parties what to do; she/he respects and trusts them enough to come up with the best-fitting resolution.

Downplaying the role of the expert is perhaps the most important of the four bases of the ReST Method in that it promotes the formation of respect, safety and trust in the process.

These concepts of building and maintaining Respect, Safety and Trust while downplaying the role of the expert provide the foundation that supports effective communication between the parties. Without the foundation, the communication between will be ineffective and insincere.

A RELAXING, MORE EFFICIENT SHORTCUT

The name "ReST Method of Conflict Resolution" implies that this should be an easy and efficient means of mediating conflicts. That is, the mediator should not be doing the hard work involved with resolving the conflict. I promise you, that is the way this works. The job of the mediator is not to resolve the conflict but rather to guide the conflicting parties to their own resolution. I don't want to give you the impression that mediation takes no time or effort. You are there to help the parties reach a resolution that works for both of them. It is the work as the guide or referee that will take up your time as mediator.

LONG AND SHORT VERSIONS

There are three versions of the ReST Method of Conflict Resolution presented here: the long version, the short version and the preschool combo version.

The long version can be learned by reading my description of a situation between two high schoolers under the heading "TEEN CENTER FIGHT". It demonstrates all the psychological concepts and methods used in all versions of the ReST Method from beginning to end. It goes in depth on each concept and shows how, why and when to use each separate tool. The long version works best during intense conflicts such as fights and longstanding disagreements that precipitate recurring problems. It is effective in lowering the reactivity of the parties in conflict as well as ensuring the same conflict doesn't arise in the future. Adults and teenagers benefit mostly from this version.

A discussion of short version can be found under "ReST METHOD SHORT VERSION: A TYPICAL SITUATION EXAMINED". The short version presupposes that your conflicting parties understand how to use many of the tools already. Exposure to these tools takes place when you are able to work daily with students in a class setting, teaching them little snippets and concepts each day. However, many times you don't have to teach these concepts. Kids tend to know the difference between right and wrong. They can figure out when their behavior is unacceptable and what the expectation is for resolution. The short version works well in the classroom, on the playground and in any situation where children play with each other. School age children (age 5 – 12) benefit mostly from this version.

Wait! Why don't we use the long version on younger populations? Shouldn't they learn the concepts at a young age so they can use them on their own when they are older?

The older the population, the more they tend to not listen to each other and, instead, work silently in their heads to spin the story their way. These conflicts turn into debates rather than attempts to resolve. As mediators, we have to re-teach effective communication and listening skills to these people as well as make them aware of other subtleties of communication such as meta-messages. The younger population tends to stay on task to resolve their issues and is too young to understand or care about things like meta-messages.

The single most compelling thing about the ReST Method of Conflict Resolution is that it does not concern itself with what happened to precipitate the problem. That is a never-ending story that could spiral back into ancient history. For example, a fight may have broken out on the playground today between Johnny and Suzie because of something Johnny said today. Suzie may have thrown the first punch today but it was because of something Johnny said earlier because of the way Suzie looked at him, because of a conversation they had yesterday, because of something Suzie heard Johnny say last week, because… The blaming process can go on and on. The mediator will never get to the bottom of who is to blame. Johnny and Suzie may not even know why they have these hurtful feelings towards each other. They just know they do.

The ReST Method gives you a break from going into the back-story of how things started. Your job is to keep the parties focused on one thing only: "What is your solution?"

That is relaxing.

Another version exists for preschool-age children that is a combination of both the long and short versions. It is separate from all other age groups and provides an opportunity to teach the basics of effective communication at an early age. I won't be discussing it in depth. Preschoolers are in a category of their own. The younger ones don't tend to hold grudges so a simple apology or hug is all it takes to end a dispute. Also, you'll notice that I discourage talking about the conflict in most age groups. Not so in preschool. These guys need the story so that they can heal. They actually benefit by telling the other person what happened and why they did it. This doesn't raise their temper at all. For older students (starting about age 5) it does no good to relive the past hurt.

Take a breath and let's summarize. What is the ReST Method? Remember three things:

1) Create respect, safety and trust
2) Take your ego out of it by not acting like an expert.
3) Focus on the solution, (not who did what to whom).

The ReST Method is rooted in the field of psychology. It is age-appropriate and useful when applied as directed. If you're interested in knowing what theories and practices support the ReST Method, they are listed at the end of the book ("THE PSYCHOLOGICAL BASIS FOR THE ReST METHOD") with short descriptions.

BUT FIRST… "PSYCHOLOGY": IT'S NOT WHAT YOU THINK!!!

    Ask any Psych 101 student the meaning of the word "psychology". What do you expect to hear? "Psych" means "mind" and "-ology" means "the study of". Right? This is the answer we've been given by years of rote learning. This is the answer you would hear from most people who weren't around at the time Freud began developing his theories back in the 1890's.

    Bruno Bettelheim, in his book <u>Freud and Man's Soul</u>, uncovers an interesting fact about the etymology of the word. Broken down, we know that "-ology" certainly does mean "the study of". It's the root of "psych" that has been switched on us, skewing much of our thought patterns, delivering us into the notion that all we are as humans can be broken down into electricity and chemicals. But I tell you that Freud knew the special truth. His writings reek of it. "Psych", is more accurately defined as "soul".

    Let that sink in for a minute. Psychology is the study of the soul. How did that get switched on us?

The second half of the 19th century was marked by huge leaps in technology. The Industrial Revolution had marred the landscape and brought the rough life of agrarian culture to a halt. People flocked to the cities to find jobs that would guarantee wealth. Simple-minded inventors, tinkerers and technicians were lionized and compensated well for reinventing the wheel, improving it time and again.

The role of the doctor in this time was less and less special, becoming as competitive as every other business. In order to get ahead in this landscape, Freud needed to make a name for himself through diligent efforts and important discoveries. As a doctor working primarily with hysterical patients Freud was in a race to discover a talking cure for mental illness to guarantee his place in medicine. The word "psychology" hadn't yet been invented but Freud was certainly writing about the workings of the "Seele" and its central role in his findings. "Seele" (pronounced SAY-lay) is German for "soul".

In America, Freud's writings piqued the interest

of doctors and the American Medical Association. A talking cure for mental illness was a hotly debated topic and one of the most sought after discoveries. Freud's methods were becoming widely used, but in America, there was a problem. Spiritism was seen as hoidy-toidy quackery pulling apart the American fabric. The modern-day equivalent is New Age philosophy with all its crystals and mystics and hidden knowledge components. In America at the turn of the century, a harsh reaction to Spiritism was the call for empirical evidence. Freud had no chance in America if his findings were grouped along with the Spiritist movement.

The American Medical Association saw the value in Freud's work. They also saw the problem with a cure that involved working on an unknown quantity that can't be heard, smelt, held, felt, seen, sensed or proven in any empirical way. The decision was made, when translating Freud's work into English, to substitute the word "mind" for "soul". In this way, the unknown, unseen quantity at least had some empirical basis in fact. Hardcore, non-Spiritists could accept the notion of a doctor working on a mind—a part of the brain –rather than a soul.

Over time the word "psychology" became synonymous with "study of the mind" and the original meaning, "study of the soul", was buried in a political drama. Freud went along with it in order to further his career and, a hundred years later, he is known as the father of Psychology. Jungian psychologists, known for their more flowery interpretation of the workings of the mind, view Freud as missing the mark by not acknowledging the special and magical side of the human, rather, forsaking it for the electrochemical processes that can be tweaked by behavior modification.

My work in conflict resolution is based upon my time on the playground and in the office with children, teens, their parents, staff and administration. I am trained as a psychotherapist with a Master's in Counseling Psychology and an emphasis in Depth Psychology. Incidentally, the word "psychotherapy", in its roughest sense refers to "treating or curing the soul". Etymologically, it can also mean "sitting with the soul".

A SOFT REMINDER

Given that the work in conflict resolution is based upon concepts tied to the field of psychotherapy, for the purposes of this writing, when I refer to any psychological concept, I am giving a soft reminder that there is something much more delicate going on in this moment. A quality that can't be empirically proven is at stake (i.e. the soul). It can be crushed or cradled with the force of our words and actions. Practicing the ReST Method of Conflict Resolution is a pledge to acknowledge this quality, host it as an important guest and sit with it as it requests.

AN OUTLINE OF THE ReST METHOD

The ReST Method consists of three main parts: *preparation*, *communication* and *resolution*. The process starts out controlled by the mediator and then gradually eases that control over to the participants. The long version contains all of the parts listed below, whereas, the short and pre-school versions are appended.

1. **<u>Preparation Phase</u>** – This is where the groundwork for communication is set. It consists of four things:

    a. Cut out all the excess
    b. Know when it's time
    c. Validate
    d. Focus on the solution

2. **<u>Communication Phase</u>** – This is the labor intensive part for the mediator. You will do four things:

    a. use open-ended questions
    b. validate each party,
    c. teach effective listening techniques,
    d. watch for meta-messages and mirroring to occur.

3. **<u>Resolution Phase</u>** – This is where the mediator steps back and allows the parties in

conflict to figure things out. A successful resolution is:

a. fair to both parties and
b. clear: able to be published or written down

TEEN CENTER FIGHT

I'm going to tell you about a conflict that actually happened. Afterwards, I will go back over the story and highlight each phase of the conflict resolution process as it applies to the story. The names, of course, have been changed.

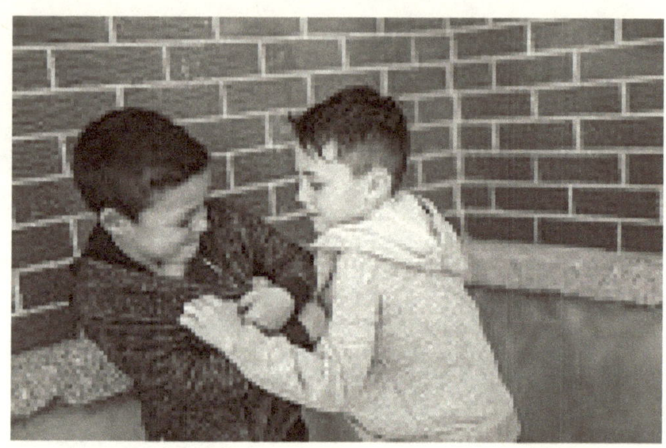

The Teen Center had a big dance on a Friday night. It was my first time as Manager of the building for such an event and I wasn't sure how these things worked yet. The dance served students in grades 6 – 9, bridging the gap between Middle School and High School, and I didn't think anything of it other than as a big fund raiser for the Teen Center. The problems I foresaw were graffiti, students running around the building where they shouldn't be, older students trying to get in and, maybe, the outside chance that a fight might break out.

I was prepared. We had extra staff hired on for the event. Volunteers from the High School were added to the staff. We had a weapons check at the front with a metal detector in case anyone tried to sneak in a knife. Staff were assigned to perform rounds in specific areas to make sure nobody was hanging out where they shouldn't be. I let my more experienced staff take the lead on this event since I wasn't out to change anything, but rather, learn from what went on. A lot of changes were going on in the department at this time and I didn't want to make more without a burning need to.

So many things went wrong that night. Kids tried to sneak in from all different areas of the building. Toilets were overflowing. Students older than 9th grade were at the dance, (all the way up to college Freshman!). Students were dirty dancing, (e.g. freaking, twerking). Staff were dancing and enjoying themselves instead of working. Worst of all, a fight broke out.

My staff, the regulars I work with everyday, jumped into action and did a great job of identifying who was actually involved. They stopped the immediate threat and separated the participants and let me know what was going on. It was apparent they had seen this before and were ready for it to happen.

This fight was between one 9th grade boy and a group of about five other boys in 9th grade and above. The boy, Robert, straight from Uganda, had a thick accent. He was well-dressed and appeared shaken, angry and vengeful beyond reason. The other group was led by DJ, a wannabe gangsta type with his hat on sideways, sagging pants, oversized shirt and a blue bandana around his head under his cap. I asked that only DJ and Robert be detained in separate parts of the building and that the other boys involved be sent home. DJ and Robert still wanted to get at each other. One sight of DJ sent Robert into a yelling rampage, pushing staff aside to get at DJ. DJ seemed much more composed and mild mannered.

I started with DJ first, telling him that he was about to solve this problem. If he were unable to solve his problem I would gladly let the police or his parents solve it. I let DJ know that I thought he was smart enough to handle this issue. After all, third graders can resolve an issue like this. I asked how he was feeling and what emotions were going through him at this point. He had a hard time describing his emotional state and would have rather told me his side of the story. I told him to wait until I spoke with Robert. DJ wanted me to hear his side the story. I told him I probably wouldn't need to hear it. I also prepared him to be 100% satisfied with the outcome of his resolution.

Robert was waiting around the side of the building with one of my staff. He couldn't see DJ but he knew he was there. Robert was still upset but had calmed down considerably. I told him the same thing I told DJ. He would decide who would handle his problem. I checked in with his emotional state as well. Robert also wanted to tell me his story. Once *again, I said I really didn't want to hear it. What I told Robert was that I expected him to handle this problem in a certain way: He and DJ would both be 100% satisfied with the outcome or we would need to let their parents or the police handle it for them.*

I did quite a bit of walking back and forth between Robert and DJ, filling them in on my expectations and preparing them for their inevitable face-to-face confrontation. My expectations were clear: This would take some time. They weren't going to fight. They would handle their situation until they were both 100% satisfied with the outcome. If they decided to quit before it was handled their parents or the police would get brought in. They weren't allowed to go back into the dance that night.

When I felt that they were both calm enough to talk I brought them just into view of each other. This stirred up some emotion with Robert so I took some time to calm him down. This gave DJ an opportunity to see just how upset Robert was. I pointed it out to DJ: "See how tense he is right now. His chest is moving up and down with big breaths. His arms are tensed. His fists are clenching. Do you think that he is ready to talk or to fight? What is his body telling you?" Sounds kind of touchy-feely, but, getting these boys to learn about body language was a huge step. I pointed out to Robert that DJ didn't look ready to fight until he enticed him with the signal of his own body. "Look how you're standing right now with your hands clenched and your body squared off to his. Your body is telling him you want to fight." When he saw that, he did the same thing. "Now relax your body and see what his does." Robert relaxed and immediately DJ let up.

I let each one know the willingness of the other to handle this situation. I asked them if they were ready to be even closer to one another. Everything I did was to get them within arms reach of each other without the threat of violence.

Once we were all close enough to talk I gave them the rules. "I'm going to give you each a chance to talk. You may not interrupt the other person even if you feel they are lying or they are making you upset. Expect what he says to make you upset. No foul language and no insults are to be directed at the other person. You are to respect each other. Absolutely no touching each other." More rules could be added as I saw fit but these were a good start.

Robert told his story first. DJ looked bored, as if he didn't care what Robert had to say. After Robert finished I asked DJ to tell me Robert's story. He couldn't. He didn't listen. We tried again. Robert told his story and, this time, DJ tried to repeat it with a few embellishments. I asked Robert if DJ had gotten his story right. Robert corrected DJ's reiteration of the story. I had DJ repeat it again until Robert approved of it. I pointed out that this wasn't a chance for each to sell me on their story, but rather, this was their chance to hear how the other experienced the problem.

DJ got to tell his side of the story to Robert. The same thing happened. Robert wasn't listening for DJ's experience of the story, but rather, wanted to correct him to what he felt was right. I made Robert re-listen to DJ's story until he could repeat it to DJ's satisfaction.

As the stories went on I would point out body language and strong words that came up during the story. I checked in with each person to ask how the other felt when that happened. I asked each how they think the other person felt at different points in the story. Everything I did was to take the temperature of the situation and to bring it out in the open. I noted when I thought they had cooled down a bit more. I compared their present emotional state to how they felt 30 minutes earlier or 5 minutes earlier. I wanted them to feel like they were making progress. (Teachers: Note how this parallels the Guided Reading experience.)

The cause of the fight was something these boys brought with them from school. DJ and his friends would make fun of Robert because he had a thick Ugandan accent. Robert was having a hard time adjusting. He ignored the insults as much as he could until he couldn't take it anymore. DJ's friends were physically assaulting Robert with little pushes and shoves at the dance and then pretending it was an accident. These boys were ganging up on Robert and Robert had no choice but to defend himself.

The resolution Robert and DJ struck was that DJ would tell his crew to back off. DJ would stop making fun of Robert. Robert would stop "eyeballing" DJ and his friends. The problem was really one-sided but it took one of them to back down so the other could lower his guard. The problem these two brought from school was never brought back to school. It ended at the Teen Center that night.

APPLYING THE ReST METHOD
PHASE ONE: PREPARATION

Occam's Razor

The first phase of the ReST Method is *Preparation*. Parties in conflict can't start resolving their issue right away. And you can't start the process until you know who is directly involved. This is where the concept of Occam's Razor is applied. This concept means to cut out all of the unnecessary elements and get it down to what really matters. Literally, you need to clear the area of all the people who aren't directly involved in the situation.

In the Teen Center fight, DJ has a group of friends backing him up. They all jumped in to "help" by telling their side of the story. That's not helpful at all. We know how people take sides. It was unlikely that an objective story would ever come out of that mess. Staff did the first part of applying Occam's

Razor by identifying who they saw was involved. I did the next part by narrowing down the incident to only two people.

In extreme cases such as fighting on a playground where a lot of people want to get involved, I apply Occam's Razor by announcing that whoever thinks they have something to do with this will be a part of the resolution process and get to share in the consequences as well. This may involve calling in parents or another authority figure. I have been able to clear a large and aggressive crowd (of about 30 participants) and narrow the problem down to only two people by making this type of announcement. Kids who thought they had something to do with the issue suddenly realize that they aren't part of it at all.

Remember: Cut out all the unnecessary parties who won't be involved in the resolution process.

Temperature and Timing

Once the field is narrowed down you need to be aware of the *temperature* of the participants. That is, "Are they so emotionally upset that they can't be near each other?" In the Teen Center fight, Robert and DJ needed to be physically out of sight of each other because Robert had to calm down. Even the thought of seeing DJ made him angry and physically upset. The best way to take the temperature of a situation is simply by talking to each party and quantifying what you want to know. "On a scale of 1 to 10, 10 being the most upset I've ever been and one being not at all, how upset are you?". Obviously a person who ranks their anger in the high levels shouldn't be next to the person they are upset with. Leave that person and ask the other person the same question. This puts more time in between the incident and the resolution. You're in no hurry and they're not ready.

Once the self-reported temperature had come down a bit, I let both parties know that they would have an opportunity to handle their issue and that this involved being in the same room with each other. As they pictured that scenario I asked: "What will it be like for you to be in the same room with that person? How upset will you be on a scale of 1 to 10?". Robert wasn't ready for a while. He tried to get out of resolving his own conflict by saying "If I ever see him again, I will kill him".

In this extreme case, I had to exert my own control over the situation. I needed them to be in the same room with each other if I were to guide them to communicate with each other. The leverage I used was a combination of parents and police involvement. In the past, the Teen Center had called the police when fights have broken out. I knew I would be held accountable by my Supervisor if this problem got bigger and I didn't call the Police. I wanted to give these guys the benefit of the doubt that they could handle this situation for themselves. I let them know their options: "If you are unable to try to solve this problem, I can call the Police to make sense of it for you. I can also call your parents and have them solve it for you. Personally, I think you are both old enough to solve this on your own." Then I added something that usually cinches up their willingness: "This is something that third graders can do. I think you are old enough to do this by yourself too, don't you?"

This sounds a little mean-spirited, telling high schoolers that someone much younger can do a better job than they can. When I work with younger groups of students I always use a grade level or two below as my leverage. For example, when my Kindergarteners are fighting I tell them that my preschoolers are able to work out their problems. It usually gets them to agree to work things out by themselves. If they don't agree to it then I know it's not time for them to do it. What's more mean-spirited: telling them that younger people can handle a similar issue or taking away their right to choose their solution? It is true that very young people can resolve their own issues. I think it takes away a person's self respect when they are deprived of their right to choose their own path.

Timing is also part of this phase. When participants have cooled down enough they will eventually commit to resolving their conflict. As the mediator, you need to be in control of the situation and direct the *when*. You need to judge when it is time for these two parties to be next to each other as well as how physically close they are able to be. You do this in two ways: 1) by stalling and putting time between the incident and 2) by checking in and taking their temperature.

The more time that goes by, the more willing participants become. Their bodies get less tense because they are removed from the heat of the issue. You can't expect people who aren't getting along to just jump into the resolution process. Sometimes one party needs more time than another to adjust.

At the Teen Center fight, the first thing I had to do was calm myself down while my staff separated the boys. Whoever is in charge of this type of meeting needs to control the situation with a cool head. How do I feel about having a fight break out at a dance that I am hosting? I'm angry with these boys. I need to get myself in a place where I can act as the role model in charge and not come across as a demeaning authority figure.

The boys were constantly getting ahead of themselves in trying to handle the situation. They would jump to conclusions about the other, whether it was the other's body language or what the other said. Don't let them get ahead of where they should be.

The boys needed time to cool down. They couldn't look at each other in the beginning. By the end of the meeting, one hour later, they were able to enter into each other's physical space and shake hands (their decision) on their own.

Remember, all wounds heal in time. Time is your greatest ally in this case. Sometimes these things need to be let go overnight or over a week. Don't ever forget about it completely. Come back to it and let them know that this isn't over. Before you let them go, let them know that they will still feel those same emotions later on but that, in time, they would go away. Sometimes when I come back from lunch, a couple students have gotten into a tussle of some kind. They can get uncooperative and refuse to participate in the resolution process. I've got a whole class of students waiting to get in the classroom and I don't have the time it would take to devote to this problem right away. I say something to the effect that we're not doing this now but we will confront this at a later time, such as: "I see that neither of you is ready to talk and work this out. That's OK… for now. But listen: you will work this out on your time tomorrow. This will not go away. Be prepared to come together and work."

My rule of thumb is that the older the participants, the less time they need to cool down since they understand what's at stake. Older participants are more willing to handle their issue in less time. However, the older participants can hurt each other more effectively and, thus, need more firm mediation. Older participants will also hold a slow-simmering grudge for a longer period of time. You've got to weigh the possible outcomes: does this need your attention right now or does it need to sit for a bit?

The younger participants don't understand as well, and will let their emotions rule their actions. The younger the child, the more time you can give them to cool off. It is less likely that younger children will continue to pursue a fight that breaks out into real danger. It is also less likely that youngsters will do lasting damage to their opponent. With young children it is all right to let them talk it out the next day. The younger child will forget what he/she was so mad about and be more willing to come up with a friendly solution.

Remember: Know the temperature of your people.

Validation

An important tool every mediator must have in their mediator's toolbox is the ability to validate the feelings of each party. This is as simple as saying something like "That must have made you very angry" when one of the parties says "He pushed me out of line".

Early in the resolution process, it is hard for a person in conflict to use words to describe all the feelings going on. Instead, they use actions that get them into trouble. A person who is emotionally hurt will try to inflict physical harm. Quid pro quo, right? As the mediator, your job is to notice where the emotion is in their words, to identify it and to bring it to light by naming it. "You must have been mortified when she said that. That really hurt you deeply." The more emotions you bring to light, the more you deflate the big balloon of anger. You also increase the amount of respect, safety and trust they feel towards you. Make sure the validation is balanced or one party will feel you are taking sides.

Listening to the story of each party is not in your job description. Listen only as a way of validating so you can gain respect and trust.

You can validate without listening too. Sometimes, when parties in conflict withhold conversation as a way of retaining control, they use body language that screams volumes. Using the discussion of *meta-messages* following this part, you will more readily be able to tell how each person is feeling. The mediator needs to take a chance and bring those feelings to the forefront. "I see that you are crossing your arms and looking away right now. You must be really angry. And your feelings must be hurt too. Is this right?"

Once you begin to name the emotions coming from their bodies, the parties will begin to open up and speak. Here, you simply paraphrase what they are saying and tag on an emotion to it if they haven't done so: "You said you hate Johnny because he hit you with a spitwad. That doesn't make you feel good inside, does it? It almost feels like he spit on you, doesn't it?. You must be really angry with him and disappointed."

Validation is a way of letting the parties know that you are not just listening to them but that you understand them on a deeper level. Leading the parties to validate each other is possible under the right conditions but is not usually the way conflicts end. It is certainly an ideal. It can be done if you are willing to enforce effective communication.

Redirect

In every case, you will need to let the participants know that they will be handling their own problem by coming up with a solution, whether it happens today or the next day. Turning their attention and focus to solving the problem, making them think about moving forward, moves their attention away from what happened in the conflict.

Think about your own experiences. Do you get upset when you think about something that upsets you? Duh! Shift their attention away from what is upsetting them. Don't let them tell you the events of the conflict, ever. You will never know what really happened. They probably don't know either. It's a waste of time. Focus on the solution. Tell them: "I don't want to hear what happened. You are here to tell me what you're going to do to solve this. When you can tell me clearly what you decide, I will listen."

Remember: You want to solve the problem, not re-live the conflict.

During the entire Preparation Phase it is important to remember that you need to be in control over the situation without being an angry authority figure. Why should you be mad? You're there to help! Remember, these are delicate entities you are working with. If your two-story house were on fire and you needed to jump into one of two safety nets, would you jump into the one being held by the firemen who say: "C'mon, idiot! Jump! What're you thinking? You're gonna burn, knucklehead!" or "Jump! You can do it! We're here for you. Everything will be all right. We won't let you fall." You would jump into either one but think about how you would feel after you're on the ground.

In summary, the preparation phase consists of four things:

1) ***Occam's Razor:*** Cut out those who are not directly involved
2) ***Temperature/Time:*** Check the emotional temperature of participants to put time between the incident and the solution
3) ***Validation:*** Reflect their feelings out loud
4) ***Redirect:*** Focus on the solution rather than the conflict.

APPLYING THE ReST METHOD
PHASE TWO: COMMUNICATION

The Communication phase of the ReST Method is when the parties in conflict come face to face and talk things out. Your goal as mediator is to have participants discuss the resolution of their conflict rather than focus on what got them into the fight in the first place. Remember, you will never know exactly why these people are at war with each other or why they need to hold on to their feelings so passionately. The only thing you can ever know for sure is how passionate they are about their side. Focusing on the problem keeps everyone in a heightened state of defensiveness, which undermines the foundation you are creating of respect, safety and trust.

I realize there are times when the story of the conflict needs to come out. This is especially important in the preschool resolution process. For whatever developmental reason, preschoolers need to hear each other's story in order to be emotionally validated. And, they haven't yet learned the art of debate, so, they aren't trying to win with a war of words. Story actually calms down the preschooler and is part of the way they lower their own temperature. It also lets time go by so the incident is not so fresh.

When an older person tells their story, it is to prove that they are right. This only serves to decrease the respect and trust between the participants. Think about it: When you have a problem with someone, do you tend to agree with all parts of their story? No. You usually reject much of what they're saying because it represents the way they see it. It's their spin on the facts. Can you trust someone like that? No. Trust diminishes in this way. Can you respect someone you can't trust? No. Respect erodes. How do you think the participants would feel about the mediator who allows this? They won't respect that kind of mediator. They can't trust that kind of mediator.

The Communication phase of the ReST Method is the longest and most involved part of the process because it represents the turning point. It's where control of the resolution process goes from the mediator to the participants. Of course, they have to be ready for it. The job of the mediator is to teach and model effective communication that will maintain the respect, safety and trust between the participants.

Learning effective communication takes time; it isn't done in a single day. I will discuss the components of effective communication below but, know this: whether or not your participants know how to effectively communicate, you can enforce effective communication without them ever being previously exposed to the concept. (See the section on "Enforcing Effective Communication" to mediate parties who don't know how to communicate effectively.

What is Communication?

I think of communication as an indirect way of experiencing. Both language and writing are ways we vicariously experience. You've heard the expressions "You had to be there" or "You just have to see it for yourself" or "Sorry you missed it" or "I want to take you to this". These are all expressions attesting to the fact that if you're not there for the experience, you can't possibly know what it's all about.

Given that spoken communication is one step removed from experience, we are, by default, at a disadvantage to thoroughly communicate the exact experience to another. Yet most of us, throughout the majority of our days, tend to communicate in haphazard ways, throwing sentences out willy-nilly, half-listening before we interrupt to talk, not really listening, yet, at the same time, making judgments. How can we maintain our relationships in this manner when our modern-day consciousness is currently being trained by the internet, TV and social institutions to take in and spit out information faster and faster? Something is getting lost. No wonder ADD and ADHD are rampant.

To keep up with the pace of society, we might need to learn how to listen and speak much in the same manner that speed-reading is done: by pulling out the kernel of the idea and glancing over the rest. Maybe someday we will be able to plug into each other's brains and download all the information we need in a flash. For business purposes, this might seem like a great solution. For human purposes this is pretty sad.

Factors of Communication

Communication is made up of two factors: inputs and outputs. Inputs are those things you observe through hearing, seeing, smelling, tasting, touching. All your senses are engaged to bring in the full experience. Outputs are the messages you deliver to another: *what* you say, *how* you say it, *how* you smell, *how* you appear, your posture, clothes, *how* you look at someone whether it's directly in the eye or not. There are so many tiny nuances in our outputs, many of them being interpreted through cultural filters, that it is important to be aware of how the communication sent may be received and perceived.

The factors of communication are at play within every interaction. They can be valuable tools if we allow ourselves to be open to them.

The point of understanding the factors that go into communication is to help us become better receivers and transmitters of our direct experiences. If you look at any face-to-face communication, there are many things that convey the message. As receivers we watch for facial expressions, hand and body gestures, posture, tone of voice, volume, word choice, agreeable statements, motive, etc. As transmitters we use these very same things to help us get our point across. The way I transmit is key to the way it will be received. And I'm not guaranteed that the way I intended my communication to be received will be experienced that way.

During the beginning of the Communication phase, the mediator retains complete control of the situation. The goal is to eventually release all control to those who are in the conflict by gradually backing out and letting those with the problem, solve their problem. Remember, it is *their* problem. You want to get out of there as soon as you can.

As a mediator, you must understand what spoken and silent messages are present in the process. You must be able to guide the parties to noticing these spoken messages and silent messages *(meta-messages)* as well. You must exert control over those spoken and silent messages. As the parties become more effective communicators you will relinquish control over to them.

VERBAL MESSAGES

The words used during the conflict resolution process can impact the temperature in the room. Harsh words tend to make us angry or tell another that we are angry. They will make the receiver defensive and less willing to participate in the process. The mediator must have control over the words spoken. You must be aware of any buzzwords that set others off. To this end, open-ended questions are an important tool to hone.

Open-ended questions are the mediator's attempt to get a response that is longer than one word. The response is meant to delve deep into the thoughts and feelings of the respondent. Open-ended questions help put time between the incident and the moment, ultimately lowering the temperature in the room. Once the mediator is able to elicit answers to open-ended questions, the process can move forward. People willing to answer in this fashion are more open and less closed off. Think of when you are in a bad mood and the type of responses you like to give. Is it a quick, bitter one-word response? Probably.

The job of the mediator is to lead both parties into hearing what the other is saying. It's hard when one of them is too angry to speak. Once both have opened up, the process can carefully move into the part of Effective Communication (see this section later) where each party shares their thoughts and feelings on the conflict. When it reaches this point, the mediator relentlessly asks the same thing over and over: "What did he/she say?" or "Repeat what she/he just said". It guides the parties into an expected pattern of behavior: listen so intently that you can repeat exactly what is being said.

But listening to the spoken messages is not even half of the communication process…

NON-VERBAL MESSAGES (META-MESSAGES)

Virginia Satir taught families how to communicate with each other by first making them aware of the silent messages they were sending to each other. These silent messages, or meta-messages, are the key to opening the door to the resolution of the conflict. I've broken them down into four major categories: *spatial, vertical, audial and gestural.* Making two conflicting parties aware of the meta-messages they are sending back and forth, as well as how those meta-messages may be received, is a large part of the work of conflict resolution.

Meta-Message Exercises

In working with meta-messages, I suggest you perform the exercises below. They are intentionally exaggerated. That is, when one person is made to be tall, the other person is likewise shortened to play up the effect and the impact of each meta-message. What you feel inside as you take part in these exercises is just a glimpse of the way all people feel when they are in conflict and silent these factors are in play.

A. Spatial or Proximal Meta-Messages

Imagine an invisible defensive shield all around yourself. When you are irritated, your bubble grows; when you are friendly, or in a good mood, your shield shrinks. We go through our days with our shield growing and shrinking without even ourselves knowing it. Sometimes our shield comes too close to someone else's shield. When that happens, our warning system goes off and we are on high alert.

In a conflict, two parties are on high alert. Your job is to bring these two parties together, closer and closer, while simultaneously shrinking their imaginary shields. There's a line you're walking here, in that, you are compromising the safety of the very people you are trying to protect from one another. Like physical rehabilitation, the patient needs to walk on the limb they've hurt in order to strengthen it. Just like physical therapy, you will need to add a little pressure, take some off; set them together, get them apart. Ease them into each other's space slowly, while you check in with them on how they're doing.

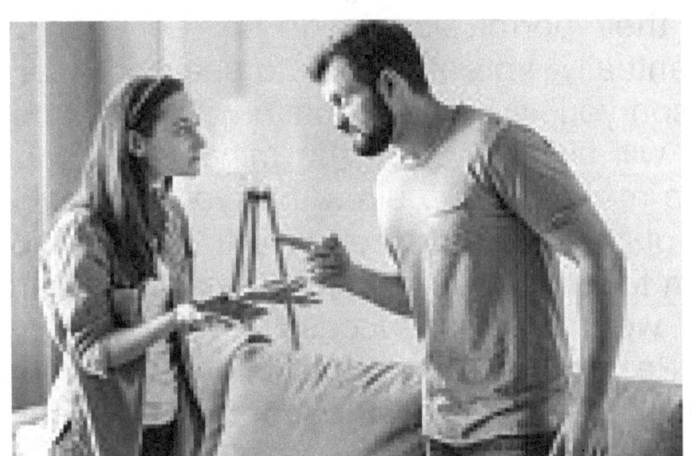

Getting too close is a silent threatening signal.

The first step to working spatial meta-messages is to answer a very specific question: At what measured distance can you bring these two people together before the threat becomes physical? Arm's distance? 10 feet? Two lovers can stand to be in each other's face all day long. That same proximity is inappropriately dangerous for people in conflict. At the same time, a distance of ten feet may be a good starting point for two sides, but it is a worthless distance from which to resolve the conflict. The leverage you hold as the mediator is key to controlling the situation and moving it through the necessary hoops as you work the meta-messages. See more on leverage.

You've adjusted the space for the conflicting parties at first by bringing them within eyesight of each other. Sometimes, that's not always the best place to start. You've got to check in with each and ask their permission to do so. Let them know that "Eventually, you are going to see and hear this other person you've had a problem with. What do you think that will be like?" Keep in mind that working spatial meta-messages requires that you move them in and out of their comfort zones with each other and get them to talk about what it's like at different distances. The work here is successful when the two parties decide for themselves that they can make their own spatial adjustments without getting physical.

Exercise:

Pair up with a partner. Start on opposite ends of a medium-size room. Ask yourself on a scale of 1 to 10 (10 being the most), "How comfortable do you feel with this person?" Now get within arm's distance of each other and ask yourself that same question. Now think of someone you don't like. Imagine that person you've paired up with is that other person. Start again from across the room and rate yourself on a scale of 1 to 10. How has that changed your feelings? How about now at arm's distance? Now, get right up close to that person so your noses touch and ask yourself that same question.

This exercise is worthless unless you do it and write down your responses. Picturing this interaction inside your head will give you some insight but actually going through the motions opens you up to the body experience. What are your hands doing? How are you standing? Are your arms crossed? Is your body squared off or turned to the side? Is your mind racing or calm? Are you sticking your chest out or are you slouching? What do these body positions mean? You've got to know what's going on inside of yourself so you can empathize with those that you are trying to bring together.

What meta-message does this couple seem to be sending to each other?

You probably noticed that you felt much more threatened in the second situation (where you are nose-to-nose) than in the first (where you are on the other side of the room). Why would you ask two sworn enemies to shake hands? Is that a likely resolution that will have an end? Would you trust this resolution?

How do you know for sure that you can bring these two parties closer? Ask them! They're the experts at how they're doing at any given moment.

Using your experience from the exercise above, help John identify what is happening in his body.

Example:

"John, you see Andy across the room there, right? On a scale of 1 to 10 how angry are you? 10 being "I just want to kill him" and 1 being "He and I are best friends right now". When you see Andy there, what do you notice is going on inside of your body? What are your hands doing? What is your heart doing? How many thoughts per second are going through your head? Close your eyes and describe everything you are feeling when you are this close to Andy."

Ask John to take a seat while you walk over to Andy and go through the same thing with him as you just went through with John.

When you're done with the first round, ask John where he is on a scale of 1 to 10 again.

"How angry are you now, John? Scale of 1 to 10. Has you anger at Andy gotten more, less or stayed the same? I want to ask you to think about something and tell me how angry you are on a scale of 1 to 10. Ready? Close your eyes and picture yourself coming within arm's distance of Andy. How angry are you? Scale of 1 to 10. What do you notice just happened in your body when I asked you to imagine that, John? What happened to your hands? Your heart? Are your thoughts racing? Notice that you are still the same distance as you were before. You're not any closer. Now, I'm going to go and talk to Andy and I want you to think about something for me: At some point, you and Andy will be within arm's distance of each other. That won't be my decision; that's up to you and Andy. You call the shots here today. Not me. You decide the outcome."

Ask John to hang out while you go through the same routine   with   Andy.

What's   going   on   here?   What   is   getting accomplished? I've just put all the power into John and Andy's hands. They know I'm not going to let them fight it out. They're safe. They also know that I'm not going to force them to do anything they're not ready for. This is both a respect issue and a trust issue. I'm just acting as a go-between while they begin   to   call   the   shots.

Spatial   meta-messages   are   those   silent messages we send telling others to stay away. When someone violates our space, we react by clenching our fists, increasing our heart rate, breathing shallow, developing a fighting stance, uttering aggressive words, and doing many other things that prepare ourselves to do battle.

B. Vertical Meta-messages

While spatial meta-messages are sent when someone invades our self-designated defense shield, vertical meta-messages are sent when someone puts himself or herself in a physical position of superiority (by hovering, standing up tall, intentionally towering over another, etc.) or inferiority (by cowering, slouching or shrinking). Think about two kids on the playground in a heated shouting match, getting in each other's face. They usually square up and stand on their tippy-toes, trying to make themselves larger and thus more threatening. Also, think about the parent or teacher telling their children to do something. The taller person usually gets their way don't they? That is, unless the smaller person can bring down the taller person with a low blow!

In every conflict, there is a proverbial battle of one-upsmanship, however, the physical reality mirrors the inner world of the combatants.

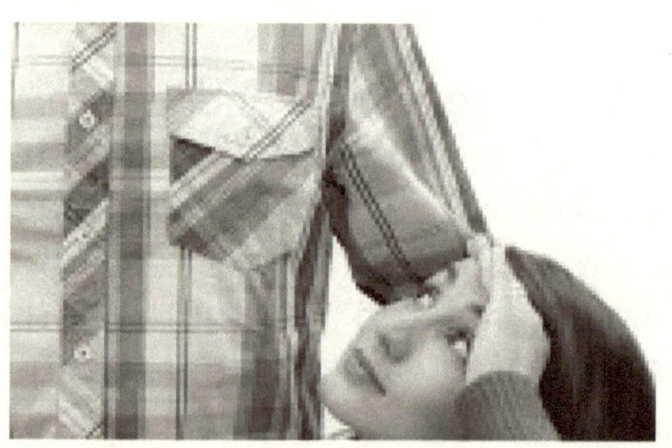

A taller person feels like they have an advantage in a conflict.

Exercise:

Pair up. One person should stand on a chair and look down at the other. If you don't have a chair to stand on, have one person kneel in front of the other. The person in the superior position should give a command such as "Pick up that book" to the person in the inferior position. Now ask the inferior "What was that like for you? On a scale of 1 to 10, (10 being most) how happy are you with that person giving the order?"

Now have the person in the inferior position give the order. Ask the same questions. Have each person note his or her personal reactions of anger. Also, note what is going on in their bodies. Are their fists clenching? Do they need to wear a certain look on their face to give an order? Is it easier to give an order from a superior position? What makes one position easier than another?

Switch positions and play it all over again. Ask the same questions. Get to know how these exaggerated positions feel.

In a conflict, one person will likely have a height advantage. That doesn't stop the shorter person from compensating. How would a shorter person likely compensate? Would they reduce the amount of space between them? Stand on their toes? Raise their voice? Threaten or use physical violence? All of the above? When you see any one of those signs of compensation, it's time to separate and check in.

Ask John: "I noticed you were beginning to raise your voice and get closer to Andy. What was going on there? Andy is a little bit taller than you and I know that sometimes when one person has a height advantage, the normal thing to do is try and raise up to their physical level. I'm going to ask that you are both sitting in chairs when we get this close again. Tell me what you think about this."

In this case I am trying to educate John and Andy about vertical meta-messages. They need to know that you will step in and take away any perceived advantage to create a level playing field so that discussions may go smoothly. You will create an enormous amount of trust by showing that you intend both parties to have the same treatment.

C. Meta-messages of Volume

Meta-messages of volume or audible meta-messages are based on how loud a person speaks.

Raising or lowering a voice can send a strong message. These are usually the first meta-messages we are consciously aware of and exert control over. Unless a person is unaware or completely devoid of social graces, you wouldn't normally yell at someone who is standing directly in front of you unless you were angry.

We learn the impact of audible meta-messages even before we can talk. As infants, we learn that crying will bring us attention, whereas, soft cooing, doesn't. When an infant wants attention, they cry until their needs are met. They don't give a whole lot more information other than "WAAAAAAAAHHHH!!!!". But, that's all we need to start checking into their needs. Do they need a bottle? Does their diaper need to be changed? Is something pinching them? Is the sun in their eyes? Do they want Mommy around? Until the parents figure out the right combination, that baby will continue to send their message.

It isn't until a child learns to finesse their communication style that they understand the underlying meaning of yelling in another person's face. Later on, we also learn about the power of an overly soft voice in a tense situation.

Try this exercise between two people:

Have two people face off and close their eyes. One person will talk in a consistent volume to the other. The person listening will give signals with their hands whether they want that person closer to them or farther away, depending only on what they feel is an appropriate distance for that volume of conversation. The mediator will help move the listener closer or farther from the talker. Of course, depending on the content of the conversation, a person may feel more threatened at a far away distance. Content is not a meta-message, but rather, an intentional message. For the purposes of this experiment have the person speak about their day or some other non-threatening topic.

When the listener is at the distance he feels is most appropriate for the volume, have him open his eyes. Note how far away they are from each other. Ask "Why does this feel like an appropriate distance?" "If you were any closer how do you think you'd feel?"

Try again using a sharp, sarcastic tone. Then again with a soft, welcoming voice. Experiment with different tones and volumes that are found in usual conflicts. Note the distance in each situation. What are you learning about appropriate volume? What are our options when one party raises their voice to the other during a mediation session?

The message being sent is that one party is not being heard. When someone isn't heard, the first adjustment they make is to raise their voice. When you see this, it's time to check in.

"Andy, I noticed you were beginning to shout at John who only stands a few feet away from you. Do you think he is having a hard time hearing you? John, I know you can hear Andy. Please tell Andy what you heard him say." Ask John to say it using the same volume Andy used. "Andy, did you have any trouble hearing John? What was it like to have John addressing you at that volume? Did you feel your temperature beginning to rise? Were you getting angry or tense in your stomach or arms?"

When you've sufficiently demonstrated that they are able to hear each other at lower volumes it is easy to transition into the Effective Listening exercises. Before you do, you should be aware of the fourth type   of   meta-message…

D. Gestural Meta-messages

It's hard for anyone to communicate without using their hands. We get into a conversation and don't even notice how much we rely on our hands to get our point across. Advisors to past Presidents have coached hand movements that are effective, demonstrative and non-threatening. I keep thinking what it must have been like to coach President George W. Bush as he explained his actions to the American people during the Iraq War. Hand movements are one form of gesture, yet we silently communicate with our whole body.

Try this:
Pair off, facing your partner. Take turns explaining to each other why you deserve a $100 dollar bill more than anyone else in the room. Pretend that the person with the best explanation gets it. When you watch another person speak, notice how they move their hands, position their body, cross or un-cross their arms, shift weight from one leg to the other, change expressions on their faces, etc. Notice how each movement or gesture makes you feel. Do you feel comfortable, threatened, surprised, engaged, interested or humiliated? What actions are they performing that you might attribute to the way you feel? What kind of movements are persuasive? What kind are comforting? What movements are threatening?

You can also demonstrate this quickly to a large group if you are able to split them up, one half on one side of a window looking in, the other half inside the room. Both groups will need to be able to see the speaker at the front of the room. Tell the group in confidence outside that they are to note the gestures and body language of the speaker as well as how those movements might be interpreted. Tell the inside group that they need to listen to the speaker and decide if he/she has persuaded them. Choose a speaker to get up in front of the group and try to convince them, within one minute, that he/she deserves a $100 dollar bill right now. When the speaker is finished, get the two groups together and compare notes. What did they notice outside where they could only see the person speaking? What did they think he/she was talking about?

As you begin to notice gestures and the feelings associated with them, you might notice your own communication style changing. During mediation, your job is to be aware of and reduce the amount of gestures and expressions that raise the temperature. There are several ways to do this. First, you can stop the conversation and bring it to the attention of the speaker. For example:

"Andy, when you're telling John how you feel about what he did to you, I see you clenching your fists and shaking them. I also see you gritting your teeth, squinching your nose and furrowing your brow like you're making a face. Do you notice that too? I wonder how it makes John feel. John, how do you feel when Andy is talking with his hands and face like that?"

Working with gestures during mediation doesn't need to go that deep. Simply being there to referee, asking either to keep their arms at their sides as necessary, will accomplish the goal of keeping the temperature at a working level.

E. Mirroring

Working with meta-messages is impactful since they are able to raise or lower the temperature of those parties involved. One interesting phenomenon that psychologists have noticed when two parties understand each other, are in synch or are hearing each other is a meta-message known as *mirroring*. Next time you have a prolonged conversation with anyone, see if you notice: Are you both holding your arms the same way? Are you standing the same way almost? Are you both sitting with one leg crossed over the other? When they change their leg-cross, do you soon change yours too? People tend to mirror or mimic each other's body language and mannerisms when they are in synch with one another. When you notice mirroring in the conflict resolution process, this is a good indicator that the two parties are getting in synch. Soon, the temperature will lower to the point where the healing can begin.

Try this:
Sit down with a friend and start a conversation about anything. Notice their body position and mirror it. If you are facing them squarely, and their right leg is crossed over their left with their hands folded neatly in their lap, you need to cross your left leg over your right and folds your hands neatly in your lap as if you were their mirror. How are you feeling? Could this be the way your friend is feeling too?

Now try this:
Next time you have a conversation longer than 5 minutes with anyone, notice if you are mirroring that person. I will sometimes catch myself in mid-mirror, that is, I notice that I change my stance sometimes to match that of the person I am speaking with. It just happens.

Meta-messages wrap-up

By working meta-messages thoroughly you are teaching people to deal with each other on an even playing field. By putting an appropriate amount of space between them, making them the same size, keeping the volume at discussion level and making them aware of their gestures, you will be able to gradually reduce your intervention and allow the temperature to raise and lower naturally. This consists of experimenting with their personal space issues first so that they don't need a table or a piece of bullet-proof glass in between them during their discussions.

EFFECTIVE COMMUNICATION

You've already laid the groundwork by cutting out the excess (Occam's razor) and making sure these two parties can come together by taking their temperature. After assessing their meta-messages and determining that they can be within arm's reach of each other, you want them to be able to talk things over (Effective Communication) and figure out how to make things better (Resolution).

First, you will need them to really hear each other's story and the emotion behind it. Using open-ended questions you will get them to open up to each other and understand their own meta-messages and temperature. This is the process of Effective Communication. Here's how it works:

1) Lay down the rules. Only one person will get to speak at a time. You (the mediator) will determine who is speaking and when. No interruptions. You are the god of this playing field and you get to determine what's fair and what's not.

2) Pick out one person to speak. Have them tell their side of the story DIRECTLY to the other person. That means they need to act as if you're not there. They won't be saying "He did this…" Instead, they'll be saying "You did this…" Make them look at each other.

3) When the first person is finished ask if there is anymore to the story to add. Offer the opportunity now so there is no need to interrupt later.

4) Ask the second person to tell you what the first person just said. This is where the frustration gets a little hotter. The second person has been waiting patiently to tell their side of the story and wants to make a few corrections about the other person's story. You don't want to give that chance. It will make the whole face-to-face meeting disintegrate. If they can't tell you what the first person just said or if the details are out of sequence it doesn't matter. Let him finish from what he remembers. Above all, don't let the first storyteller interrupt to correct the other.

5) Now ask the second person what was noticeable about the storyteller's body language. "What kind of *meta-messages* were being sent?"

6) Once the second person has re-told the first story and assessed the body language, offer a chance to add anything that may have been left out.

7) Turn back to the original storyteller and ask him to explain what was left out of the re-telling of the story.

8) Once this is done ask him how he felt when the actual incident was happening. What was going on inside his head. His body? Were his fists clenched then?

9) Ask him how he felt when he got to tell his story to the person he was having a problem with. What was going on inside his mind and body then?

10) Ask how he feels right now.

11) Turn to the second person and ask him how the other person described his feelings at each point in time. Ask if he noticed the first person's body language.

12) Ask the second person to tell his story now and repeat steps 2 through 10 for him.

If the parties can't cooperate with the process you must be prepared, as the mediator, to take absolute control of the situation. Eventually the back and forth of listening, repeating and checking-in becomes easier and the two parties can take over by themselves. You may need to remind them of the leverage you have to make it happen. It doesn't need to go on for very long. They may have a lot they want to say to each other and they may have heard enough. Once they have demonstrated this ability, you are ready to hand over the reins of hammering out the actual resolution. That is, the agreement they will both honor in order to have peace in their relationship.

The "e" in ReST

It's time to have a discussion about the lower case "e" in the ReST Method. I didn't mean to imply that this is a three-legged stool of respect, safety and trust, upon which rests my theory. I also didn't want to give the impression that it's not as important as developing Respect, Safety and Trust. I think it makes the word stand out more written in this way. But, the big reason for the small "e" is to have a visual reminder of the most important concept in this book. You can take it as one of two things. First, you can think of it as downplaying the role of the "expert". Or you can use it as a reminder to get your "ego" out of the way.

As a side note, remembering the discussion of the word "psychology" and how it really means "study of the soul", I like to think of the word "resolution" as "re*soul*ution" instead. This process really does lead participants to tend to the soul of each party. It's a deep and caring process if done right. The crushing presence of an overbearing authority figure with all the answers, as well as being the dealer of the consequences, will scare away the gentle presence of soul. To preserve the delicate balance that leads to buy-in towards a true resolution, you've got to act more like a coach than an expert. Your role is to help the parties in conflict discover their most effective solution rather than dictate the wants and needs that you think will fit.

The resoulution is the most empowering part of the process. There really isn't that much to it. This is where the mediator acts more like a guide. You provide structure while the participants provide the solution.

What does this "structure" look like? Didn't we just go through a whole thing about not being too rigid? Isn't structure kind of defeating that idea? Think of it like the Autopia cars at Disneyland. You, as mediator, are the staff who makes sure each passenger is buckled into the car safely. The parties in conflict are in charge of the accelerator, the brake and the steering wheel. Remember that Autopia has a track-line down the middle that keeps the car on the road so that each trip is successful? In the same way, the mediator provides a place and a presence for the process to resolve.

APPLYING THE ReST METHOD
PHASE THREE: RESOULUTION

Resoulution is the result or the end product of the process. There is an expectation that something must come out of the work that both parties are doing and it must be tangible. They must be able to clearly express the outcome they have reached. Many times, with my Kindergarten and first graders, when I ask what the solution is I hear: "We said 'sorry' to each other." We all know this a simply an expectation from authority figures that's been overused (i.e. "say 'sorry' to each other and don't let it happen again"). That may be a solution but it isn't always what both parties want. Apologies are usually insincere and don't do much to curb the conflict from happening again.

We need to know that the solution satisfies both parties as closely to 100% as possible. Without taking up hours of frustrating time, how is that possible? My answer is to leave it up to the participants.

This is not your problem as a mediator. Your job is to make sure these two are ready to solve *their* problem. It is *their* problem. You must remind them of this until they take the lead on it. I'm reminded of a part in one of M. Scott Peck's books (maybe *The Road Less Travelled*) where he goes to his supervisor for guidance and says "I have a problem". His supervisor only responds with "It sounds like you do have a problem", which frustrates him to no end. Peck was looking for advice, but instead got shut down. It took him awhile before he figured out that his supervisor was telling him that no matter how much advice he would hear, the solution to his problem was only going to be satisfying if it came from himself. Gray had some work to do and realized what a favor his supervisor had done by forcing him to confront the solution in his own way.

Your parties in conflict need to understand this in no uncertain terms. This is not *your* problem; this problem belongs to them. They are the only ones who can fix this because they are the only ones who know the entire history of the problem. They know the ins and outs of who did what and when it happened. They know how much validation they need from the other and what their expectations are of each other. Whether they can say it or not is another issue. But, it must be entirely up to them to come up with a solution that fits their unique situation. The solution must make sense to both of them and they must be able to communicate it in very specific terms.

The way I like to make this happen is a lot like getting into a cold pool during a hot summer day. If you get in a little bit at a time, it will take a lot longer to get used to the water temperature. If you force yourself to dive in or get pushed in, splash around a bit and forget that the water is super-cold, you tend to get used to it faster.

The "push" I give to my students goes something like this… I tell them: "*You* are going to come up with the solution. I am not going to solve this for you because I can't; I will get it wrong. You are only going to tell me what the solution is. You are not going to tell me who did what because that is not a solution, that is a restatement of the problem. You are no longer focusing on the problem; you are only focusing on the solution. The solution is the thing that you want out of it. You must clearly state the outcome each of you wants. The outcome is the one thing that will make you drop the problem forever. Your partner must be able to repeat it back to you. It must be something that the other person will agree to. It must be something that works for both of you."

This is an eye-opener for many in conflict, much like getting pushed into a cold pool. People are not used to being told that they will solve their problem. So many are used to bringing their problems to a judge, stating their case and letting the judge decide. I realized early on that playing that role always left someone unhappy. In addition, I had to stop what I was doing to hear each side of the story and make sense of the details before coming to a judgment. This inevitably leads to a shouting match, angers flaring up and the problem not really being solved to anybody's satisfaction.

Place and Presence

As discussed earlier, try not to think of it as preparing the way for their resolution process, rather, think that you are providing partial structure for a discovery. The structure is the total experience that allows for honest communication to happen in a safe place. You only need to offer a place. The place may be in a quiet classroom during recess time when all the other students are on the yard. It may be in an office down the hall from the rest of their peers. It may be in a designated part of the playground on the school campus where yard-duty staff can see from a distance.

You also need to make yourself available. The presence or lack of presence of the mediator is up to the participants. They will let you know how much of you they need with their words or actions. A mediator that is present can guide the process when it gets off track or starts to heat up again. A mediator that isn't present just needs to hear the end result of the resolution and ask "Are you both completely satisfied? Are you happy with this outcome?"

A successful solution is:
-fair to both parties
-able to be clearly stated, published or written down

The resoulution doesn't need to make sense to the mediator as much as it needs to address the needs of the parties in conflict. It is true that in some cases, the mediator has the obligation to some sort of follow-up. For example, when one student steals from another and they decide on a solution that makes them both happy such as "He gave me back my toy and promised he wouldn't steal from me again", the mediator still needs to reinforce the idea that stealing is wrong and that it hurts others. In another example where one student is bullying another and the solution is that the bully will apologize and not bully the other person, the mediator has a responsibility to address the bullying.

At this point, notice how fully empowered your parties in conflict are. You have provided the structure but they are providing the solution. You have fully moved from controlling the situation to giving that control over to the participants. You've gone from being the driver to now acting as tour guide. Someone else is driving while you are making light-hearted comments about the scenery.

PHYSICAL SPACE CONSIDERATIONS

Traffic in Los Angeles is legendary. On the 10 Freeway in particular, there is something that I've seen nowhere else called an Accident Investigation Site (AIS). The defined purpose of an AIS is to get an accident off the freeway, out of the flow of traffic to carry out the collision investigation. It's a great idea not just to get the collision out of traffic but because looky-loos cause much of the traffic on the freeways—when there's an accident, everyone slows down to look.

We know that conflicts tend to arise in play spaces when children are present. We even have a lot of good information on how to teach conflict resolution. What we don't have is a type of infrastructure to address the need. The AIS holds a clue for what we need to do for those in conflict: get those involved out of the way, so the larger population can resume the activity. For this to happen, we need a dedicated, separate space for conflict resolution on every playground.

So, what might it look like if a play space were designed to address the needs of patrons who need to resolve a conflict?

I've heard of dedicated spaces set aside in the corner of a playground with a "Rainbow Bridge" theme. Parties in conflict stand at opposite ends of the bridge and start by stating their view of the problem. Once they state the problem to each other they take one step forward. On the next step they say how it made them feel. They take another step forward. On the next space they state what they would like to happen. They take another step forward and end up in the same space where they make the wish of the other come true. Here's an example:

P1: *(standing on RED)* "You keep hitting me."

P2: *(standing on VIOLET)* "You keep calling me names."

Both take a step forward.

P1: (standing on ORANGE) "When you hit me it makes me feel sad."

P2: (standing on INDIGO) "When you call me names it makes me angry."

Both take a step forward.

P1: *(standing on YELLOW)* "I want you to promise to stop hitting me."

P2: *(standing on BLUE).* "I want you to promise to not call me names anymore."

Both take a step forward to the final space (GREEN) and agree to each other's terms or agree to start over again.

ReST METHOD SHORT VERSION:
A TYPICAL SITUATION EXAMINED

Many situations arise in a classroom or after-school childcare setting that happen again and again. Teachers and staff know how to handle these situations because they have already encountered many of these situations before. They have a headful of perfected responses through years of trial and error. But young students don't have the years of experience that adults do in managing, navigating and compromising these seemingly small altercations. To an adult it's no big thing. To a child, it is the *only* thing. Children need experience with solving their own altercations. How else will they learn the art of conflict resolution? And teachers could use a break from having to solve all those problems, right?

Below is a sample of something a teacher might encounter everyday.

Student 1: *Cece is bothering me. She keeps copying everything I do.*

Student 2*: Jala is being mean to me. She told me to 'shut-up'.*

The teacher has options: handle it her/himself or let the students figure it out. What do they learn from the teacher figuring it out for them? For example,

Teacher: *"Jala, don't say 'shut-up'; it's not nice and it hurts feelings. Cece, stop copying Jala. She doesn't like it."*

Here the teacher acts like a translator for things the students could have told each other directly. The students feel both validated and shamed because they saw their friend get reprimanded but they also got reprimanded themselves. The students will keep coming back to the teacher because that is the authority figure who knows how to handle everything. Students don't learn how to self-advocate.

Here's something else a teacher might do in that same scenario:

Teacher: *"Cece, why are you copying Jala? Can't you see she doesn't like it? I need you to stay away from her until you can play nicely without copying her. Jala, why did you say 'shut-up'? That's not nice, is it? We don't use those words. We say 'be quiet' or 'stop' instead.*

The question 'why' is not easy for anyone at any age to answer. Why do we ask it? It's just easy… automatic. It doesn't get the kids thinking. Instead, it makes them feel shame. The teacher decides the outcome for the students by separating them until they can play nicely. Who decides when that is? Chances are, the students won't give it a second thought and will start playing with each other immediately. Also, the teacher's attempt to instruct by saying "We don't use those words. We say this instead…" is a lame attempt at instruction.

In both these knee-jerk reactions, the adult is acting like the all-knowing authority figure rather than a coach. This is meatball surgery on the battlefield. The stitches hold for now until the patient can get to a real hospital.

As mediators, we want to get away from solving the problems and instead act more like a guide. It's Sherlock Holmes versus Columbo. Sherlock would uncover all the details and arrive at a perfect conclusion after a long and painstaking process. We don't have that time and a problem between kids just isn't going to hit the headlines. In addition, there is still a chance that the students think your decision is unfair and then you will have to answer to their parents who only believe their child's side of the story. Down the rabbit hole we go!

When mediating a conflict, act more like Columbo instead of Sherlock.

Wouldn't you rather take all of this responsibility and shift it to someone else?

In the 1970s, a popular TV show was "Columbo", starring Peter Falk as a seemingly bumbling, unobservant detective. Columbo would get assigned to a case and let the smug perpetrator incriminate him/herself. Columbo never seemed to find a lot of evidence. He just asked the right question at the right time. The perpetrator would always have an a-ha moment at the end when they realize Columbo wasn't inept after all.

An effective mediator is more like Columbo. You're not looking for evidence or turning over stones to get at the truth. You act like you know nothing about what's going on. I always like to say, "I don't know how to solve this problem" or "If you let me solve this problem, I'm going to get it wrong". And it's true. I can never know who really said or did a mean act first that eventually led to the altercation we have now. There's always going to be something that came before…

"He told me to shut-up"
"Because she was copying me"
"Because he wouldn't let me play with my friend"

"Because he and I were playing together first"
"Because you told him not to play with me"
"Because you were mean to me"
"Because you were talking about me"
"Because you looked at me funny"
"I did not"
"Yes you did and then you…"

It goes on and on into ancient history. Real or imagined. And it just doesn't matter. None of it. What really matters is that they get beyond the "what happened" phase and into the "what's next" phase. Focusing on the details of the conflict is reliving the conflict and raises the temperature. Columbo would never ask "What happened?" He only concerned himself with the solution. Your only focus in the conflict resolution process is getting your parties in conflict to focus on the solution.

Let's replay the scenario:

Student 1: *Cece is bothering me. She keeps copying everything I do.*

Student 2: *Jala is being mean to me. She told me to 'shut-up'.*

Teacher: *"I need the two of you to do me a favor. I am not really good at things like this and I wasn't there to see who did what. But you two were. You are the experts here. So, here's what I need you to do: you are both going to sit here away from everyone else and you are going to come up with a solution to your problem. When you figured out a solution that you will be 100% happy with (pointing to Student 1) and you are also 100% happy with (pointing to Student 2), come and let me know.*

Within minutes, my students will have a solution that usually involves saying 'sorry' to each other or promising not to do an undesirable behavior again.

But sometimes…

Student 1 and 2: *"We can't figure it out!"*

This is when I use leverage…

Teacher: *"OK. Do you promise to do what I decide for you? I might say not to ever play with each other again. Or I might decide that you both have to sit in the office during recess. I just don't know until I hear every detail. I'm not really good at this."*

Or…

Teacher: *"Who would be a good judge to decide what happens to both of you? Your parents? The Principal? What kind of consequences do you think they might decide for you? Never play with each other again? Stay away from each other? Write apology notes to each other?"*

Notice that I'm really pushing for them to choose to work on the solution. Eventually, everybody does.

WHAT DO YOU WANT?

But how does a student know how to solve a conflict that they've never had experience with before? It's easier for kids to solve something that they have practical experience with (e.g. a friend hits them, a friend says something mean) but when they encounter something for the first time (e.g. another person comes in and takes their friend away to play separately), they have no idea how to solve it.

This is where the mediator needs to step in and, continuing to play the role of Columbo, says:

"What do you want to happen?" (to Student 1) and *"What do you want to have happen?"* (to Student 2).

Student 1: *"I want Sara to play with me."*

Student 2: *"I just want to play with Juhi sometimes."*

Ouch! Student 1 doesn't want to hear that. She's been best friends with Student 2 since Pre-School. How dare she have other friends! This is where the mediator needs to step in and make sure they've heard each other.

Teacher: *"I hear that you (Student 1) want to play with Sara and you (Student 2) sometimes want to play with Juhi. Is that correct? Say that to each other."*

Student 1: *"I want you to play with me."*

Student 2: *"I want to play with you AND I want to play with Juhi, sometimes, too."*

Teacher: *"I keep hearing the word 'sometimes'. I wonder if you two need to figure out a way to make you both happy."*

I can't imagine a scenario where the students don't try to push this back to the teacher to solve. The job of the teacher as a mediator is to keep bumping them back on the road to their solution. Use "I wonder…" statements and remind them that any solution you come up with is not going to be the best idea. Offer some crazy ideas to demonstrate:

Teacher: *"What if you (Student 1) sit on a bench on days when she plays with Sara. And how about you (Student 2) can only eat dog food for snack on days you play with Sara. I wonder if that would be a good solution?"*

Of course not! They can see you are not good at this. But that is your best solution so maybe you shouldn't be solving kids' problems.

The big idea is to not let the parties in conflict focus on the past. They must be directed to the future where the solution is. Also, don't let the parties in conflict trick you into solving their problem for them. Keep pushing it back on them. And when communication begins to break down, refer back to the Effective Communication guidelines. Directly instruct them to listen to each other, one at a time, repeating what the other said, and checking their temperature.

Here are the big idea takeaways:

-Keep the focus on the solution, not the conflict details
-Let the parties in conflict solve the problem
-Guide them to hear what the other wants

MEDIATOR INSIDE THE CONFLICT

When you have a good grasp of conflict resolution as a mediator you may notice that you aren't really using these techniques and ideas in your own interpersonal conflicts. When arguing with your spouse, co-worker, peer, etc. and it gets nasty, are you able to refer back to any of these concepts and apply them? It is hard to be inside the conflict and attempt to be a mediator as well. This book is dedicated to mediating conflicts as an outsider. When you are one of the parties in conflict how will you use the ReST Method? Can you be both mediator and party in conflict? Or will you need to bring in an outside mediator?

Take a step back. What are you asking parties in conflict to do? They are told not to focus on the problem. They are told to focus on a solution. That is what you should be doing as well.

Think about it.

You are in an argument with another (e.g. your spouse, an administrator, a peer, a colleague). Take yourself out of argument mode. Turn off the blame statements. Do what it takes to lower your own temperature. Ask yourself "What is it I'm trying to accomplish?" "Is this something this person can give me?" "Will it make me happy?" Now, ask them for it.

EPILOGUE

Imagine if we could go back in time to when the Middle East crisis was said to have its beginnings with Isaac and Ishmael. If these two could have seen the damage their problem caused their descendants, do you think they might have worked things out on their own? Imagine if we were to push away all the people who have nothing to do with the original argument and were able to make only the two half-brothers sit down until they figured out a solution that they would both be happy with. Could they have focused on a solution and not relive the problem over and over?

Now come back to reality in the present day, seeing yourself as a mediator. Are the daily conflicts you encounter any less important? I don't mean to compare the problems between two kids on the playground to the problems in the Middle East. I mean to say that we, as mediators, have a responsibility to teach conflict resolution skills. We need to work with young populations and entrust/empower those youngsters with outcomes that make them happy. As these kids grow up, they will be solution-oriented rather than detail-oriented debaters focused only on winning their argument. After all, winning the argument does not end the conflict. It tends to only make one person in the conflict happy.

THE PSYCHOLOGICAL BASIS FOR THE ReST METHOD

The ReST Method is informed by a variety of tested and well-known theories and ideas (below in bold) that you may know from the field of Psychology.

Generalization - The mediator goal attempts to minimize impact of a negative statement by stating how this type of thing happens everyday. For example, a person says "I don't have any friends". The mediator can generalize this to make it sound like a problem many students have (e.g. "There are a lot of students in your grade who feel like that" or "I hear that a lot from people your age").

Hierarchy of Needs - Maslow's maintained that a person needed to accomplish a certain level before they could move on to the next. Therefore, a person's PHYSIOLOGICAL needs (e.g. air, food, sex, etc.) must be met before they could begin to feel safe. Once physiological needs are met, SAFETY needs must be met, then SOCIAL needs, EGO needs, and finally SELF-ACTUALIZATION can occur. The mediator provides for the safety needs, social needs and ego needs in the resolution process.

Meta-messages - Virginia Satir was a pioneer of family-centered therapy. She taught families how to communicate with each other by first making them aware of the silent messages they were sending to each other. These silent messages, or *meta-*

messages, are the key to opening the door to the resolution of the conflict. I've broken them down into four major categories: spatial, vertical, audial and gestural. Making two conflicting parties aware of the meta-messages they are sending back and forth, as well as how those meta-messages may be received, is a large part of the work of conflict resolution. Working with meta-messages can have explosive effects since they are able to raise or lower the temperature of those parties involved. Much more on meta-messages will be covered later.

Mirroring - This is an automatic and mostly unnoticed response to watch for. When this happens, it means the two parties in conflict are on the same wavelength, that they are communicating and feeling the same way. It is a positive sign that things are lightening up between them. Mirroring is when you see both people in roughly the same physical stance as if they were mirrors of each other. For example, one person has their left hand in their lap, their right hand on the table behind them and they are slouching in their chair with their right foot crossed over their left knee. The other person might be doing the exact same thing or they have their hands and legs reversed as in a mirror.

Motivational Interviewing - Open-ended questions, affirmations, reflective statements and summaries are all ways that the mediator can control the pace and temperature of the process. When students are reactive and short-tempered, asking closed-ended "yes" or "no" questions gives in to their anger. The use of *open-ended questions* that get them to talk will help a person breathe more evenly, get their mind off their anger and reduce their reactivity. An *affirmation* is a statement that says "you are getting stronger" or "you are getting good at this process". Affirmations help them feel good about themselves, lowering reactivity. *Reflective statements* are guesses about a person's emotional state such as "this seems to make you angry" or "you seem to be much more calm now". They help to show a person how they are progressing emotionally during the process. Many times, a child is unable to describe their emotional state beyond being "mad". *Summaries* help shorten the list of grievances against another person and put them into a smaller package in order to deal with it and diminish its effect on the person. For example, a person keeps saying that another person keeps hitting, spitting, name-calling and badgering them. Rather than continuing to go through their list, the mediator balls them up into "these things that bother you". This removes the person from focusing on the actions and directs them to some non-descript actions instead.

Neuro-linguistic programming - Sometimes the mediator needs to insert the language of success into the vocabulary of those in conflict. Simply by having them say "I can do this" or "I am focusing on a resolution that works for me" is a powerful method.

Occam's razor: When a conflict is fresh, everyone wants to get into the act. Friends support each other (e.g. "I saw exactly what happened") and want to offer their "help". A big crowd makes conflict resolution impossible. As mediator, you need to cut out all the unnecessary people and get it down to the two people who have the problem with each other.

Operant Conditioning - B.F. Skinner popularized this form of treatment in the field of Behavioral Psychology. He showed that, through repetition and the right stimuli, you could train anyone to do anything. In the ReST Method, you will be re-training students to focus on the resolution rather than the conflict by using leverage. You will not be providing shocks to discourage arguments!

Psychodynamic Psychiatry – Psychodynamic Psychiatry is the field of Psychology that takes into account the environment a person lives in as well as the developmental stage to explain their behavior. In this sense, the mediator needs to take into account the developmental and environmental issues of the parties in conflict. If one person has an unfair advantage over the other and can force a favorable resolution, the mediator will need to act on behalf of the weaker party.

Reframing: This is when the mediator reflects back what was said with a positive spin without invalidating it. For example, a person who says "nobody likes me" needs to hear something different before they create this reality. The mediator could say something like "you're not feeling too popular right now".

Rubberband theory - John Gray proposed this theory in his book <u>Men Are From Mars, Women Are From Venus</u>. He states that the further away someone gets from you, the closer you want to be to them. Likewise, the closer they get, the farther away you want to be. In the conflict resolution process, people in conflict have this invisible space that they are comfortable with. When one retreats, the other attacks. The mediator must be there to help determine what is the appropriate physical space between the parties in conflict.

Soulwork - neo-Jungian psychologists believe, just as Freud originally intended, that the therapist is treating the soul rather than the mind of an individual. Keeping this in mind should help the mediator focus on treating her/his students with respect while trusting them to resolve their conflicts and providing them a safe place.

Self-fulfilling prophecy – Just as in neuro-linguistic programming above, what is stated in the resolution process as fact can sometimes become true. If someone says "You always pick on me", that person can expect to be picked on after the process if the statement isn't changed or added to (e.g. "You always pick on me and it makes me feel sad".)

Self Psychology - Kohut introduced the ideas of validation, reframing and generalization. During the resolution process the mediator may need to take charge of the language used by those in conflict to maintain the respect, safety and trust in the room. *Validation* occurs when the mediator notices something that is unspoken in the session (e.g. "I see you are trying really hard to work on a resolution" or "This really upsets you"). It makes the parties in conflict feel like they are heard or understood. *Reframing* is necessary when a hurtful or thoughtless remark is made (e.g. "He always does this to me") and the mediator changes it to "He does this to you often"). *Reframing* is meant to soften harsh statements to keep the temperature low. *Generalization* happens when the student makes a negative statement (e.g. "I suck at Math") and the mediator changes it to demonstrate that they aren't the only ones in this situation (e.g. "Math is hard for a lot of people"). Generalization makes the action seem like anybody is capable of having these feelings, not just this person.